I0448424

NOV. 02

A Method to Assess the Vulnerability of
U.S. Chemical Facilities

NCJ 195171

Sarah V. Hart

Director

Findings and conclusions of the research reported here are those of the author(s) and do not reflect the official position or policies of the U.S. Department of Justice.

This study was conducted by Sandia National Laboratories under Interagency Agreement 1997–LB–R–007.

The National Institute of Justice is a component of the Office of Justice Programs, which also includes the Bureau of Justice Assistance, the Bureau of Justice Statistics, the Office of Juvenile Justice and Delinquency Prevention, and the Office for Victims of Crime.

Nov. 02

A Method to Assess the
Vulnerability of U.S. Chemical Facilities

NCJ 195171

Foreword

This special report presents an overview of a prototype methodology to assess the security of chemical facilities within the United States. This vulnerability assessment methodology identifies and assesses potential security threats, risks, and vulnerabilities and guides the chemical facility industry in making security improvements.

The National Institute of Justice developed the vulnerability assessment methodology in collaboration with the Department of Energy's Sandia National Laboratories. Sandia National Laboratories employees are recognized experts in security and counterterrorism and have extensive experience in the protection of nuclear weapons and radiological materials. Sandia National Laboratories has developed vulnerability assessment methodologies for other critical infrastructure components, including dams, water treatment and supply facilities, and correctional facilities.

During the development, testing, and validation of the assessment methodology, National Institute of Justice and Sandia National Laboratories staff—

- Collected and reviewed information relevant to the threats, risks, and vulnerabilities associated with chemical facilities, including current security practices in the chemical industry.

- Held meetings and discussions with a range of industry, government, and citizen representatives, as well as private individuals.

- Created an online site to describe the development effort and solicit comments.

- Inspected chemical facilities.

The use of the vulnerability assessment methodology is limited to preventing or mitigating terrorist or criminal actions that could have significant national impact—such as the loss of chemicals vital to the national defense or economy—or could seriously affect localities—such as the release of hazardous chemicals that would compromise the integrity of the facility, contaminate adjoining areas, or injure or kill facility employees or adjoining populations. It addresses physical security at fixed sites but not cyber and transportation security issues. Related information on these issues can be found at the National Institute of Justice Web site, *http://www.ojp.usdoj.gov/nij.*

The National Institute of Justice appreciates the substantial cooperation of chemical industry representatives who provided invaluable access and assistance in the development of this vulnerability assessment methodology. This project also benefited from the suggestions of other Department of Justice components, the Office of Homeland Security, the Department of Energy, the Environmental Protection Agency, the Department of Transportation, numerous organizations, and private citizens. This cooperative effort has produced a useful and reliable methodology for improving the security of our Nation's chemical facilities.

Sarah V. Hart
Director
National Institute of Justice

Overview of the Prototype VAM

The prototype Vulnerability Assessment Model (VAM) developed for this project is a systematic, risk-based approach in which risk is a function of the severity of consequences of an undesired event, the likelihood of adversary attack, and the likelihood of adversary success in causing the undesired event. For the purpose of the VAM analyses:

Risk is a function of S, L_A, and L_{AS}
S = severity of consequences of an event.
L_A = likelihood of adversary attack.
L_S = likelihood of adversary attack and severity of consequences of an event.
L_{AS} = likelihood of adversary success in causing a catastrophic event.

The VAM compares relative security risks. If the risks are deemed unacceptable, recommendations can be developed for measures to reduce the risks. For example, the severity of the consequences can be lowered in several ways, such as reducing the quantity of hazardous material present or siting chemical facilities (CFs) farther from populated areas. Although adversary characteristics generally are outside the control of CFs, they can take steps to make themselves a less attractive target and reduce the likelihood of attack to their facilities. Reducing the quantity of hazardous material present may also make a CF less attractive to attack. The most common approach, however, to reducing the likelihood of adversary success in causing a catastrophic event is increasing protective measures against specific adversary attack scenarios.

Because each undesirable event is likely to have its own consequences, adversaries, likelihood of attack, attack scenario, and likelihood of adversary success, it is necessary to determine the risk for each combination of risk factors.

Although the VAM is usually used for some or all CFs that are required to submit risk management plans (RMPs), it can also be used for undesired events of lesser consequence than those found in RMPs.

The VAM has 12 basic steps:
1. Screening for the need for a vulnerability assessment.
2. Defining the project.
3. Characterizing the facility.
4. Deriving severity levels.
5. Assessing threats.
6. Prioritizing threats.
7. Preparing for the site analysis.
8. Surveying the site.
9. Analyzing the system's effectiveness.
10. Analyzing risks.
11. Making recommendations for risk reduction.
12. Preparing the final report.

A more detailed discussion of the VAM steps is found in later sections.

VAM Flow Chart

The 12 steps are described in the following flowchart (exhibit 1), and a detailed explanation of each step follows the chart.

Exhibit 1. Vulnerability Assessment Methodology for Chemical Facilities Flowchart

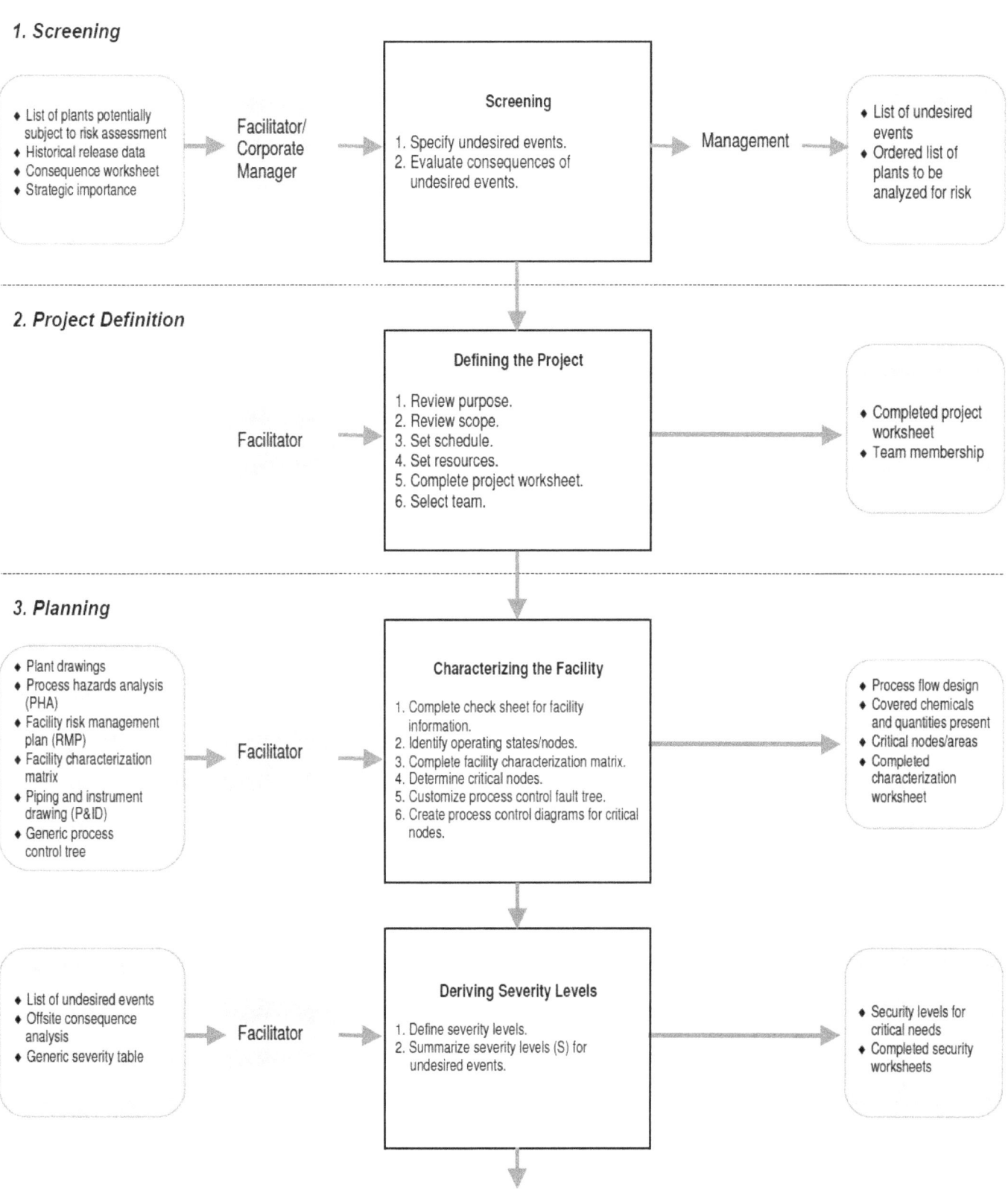

1. Screening

- List of plants potentially subject to risk assessment
- Historical release data
- Consequence worksheet
- Strategic importance

→ Facilitator/ Corporate Manager →

Screening
1. Specify undesired events.
2. Evaluate consequences of undesired events.

→ Management →

- List of undesired events
- Ordered list of plants to be analyzed for risk

2. Project Definition

Facilitator →

Defining the Project
1. Review purpose.
2. Review scope.
3. Set schedule.
4. Set resources.
5. Complete project worksheet.
6. Select team.

→

- Completed project worksheet
- Team membership

3. Planning

- Plant drawings
- Process hazards analysis (PHA)
- Facility risk management plan (RMP)
- Facility characterization matrix
- Piping and instrument drawing (P&ID)
- Generic process control tree

→ Facilitator →

Characterizing the Facility
1. Complete check sheet for facility information.
2. Identify operating states/nodes.
3. Complete facility characterization matrix.
4. Determine critical nodes.
5. Customize process control fault tree.
6. Create process control diagrams for critical nodes.

→

- Process flow design
- Covered chemicals and quantities present
- Critical nodes/areas
- Completed characterization worksheet

- List of undesired events
- Offsite consequence analysis
- Generic severity table

→ Facilitator →

Deriving Severity Levels
1. Define severity levels.
2. Summarize severity levels (S) for undesired events.

→

- Security levels for critical needs
- Completed security worksheets

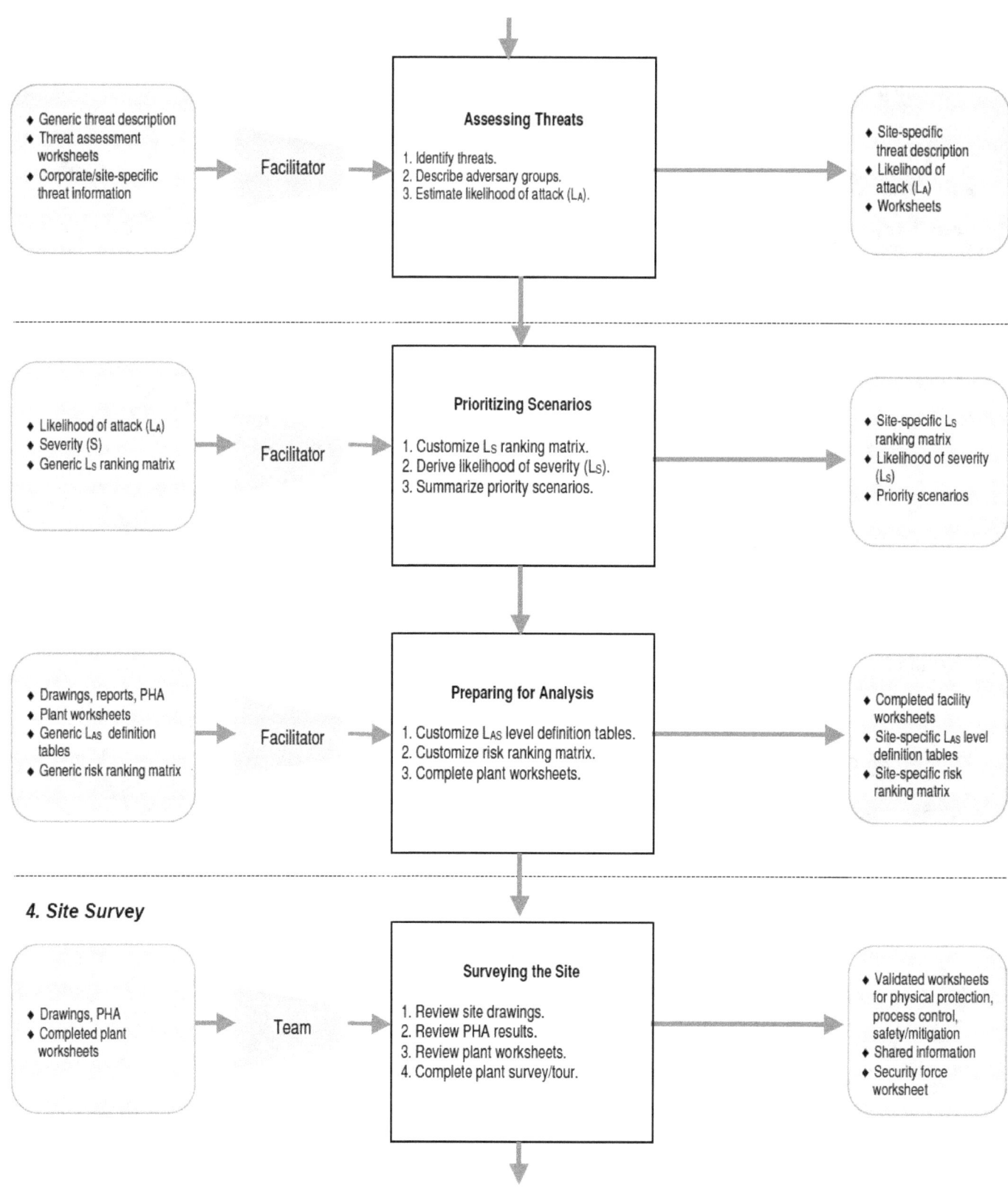

Assessing Threats

1. Identify threats.
2. Describe adversary groups.
3. Estimate likelihood of attack (L$_A$).

- Generic threat description
- Threat assessment worksheets
- Corporate/site-specific threat information

Facilitator

- Site-specific threat description
- Likelihood of attack (L$_A$)
- Worksheets

Prioritizing Scenarios

1. Customize L$_S$ ranking matrix.
2. Derive likelihood of severity (L$_S$).
3. Summarize priority scenarios.

- Likelihood of attack (L$_A$)
- Severity (S)
- Generic L$_S$ ranking matrix

Facilitator

- Site-specific L$_S$ ranking matrix
- Likelihood of severity (L$_S$)
- Priority scenarios

Preparing for Analysis

1. Customize L$_{AS}$ level definition tables.
2. Customize risk ranking matrix.
3. Complete plant worksheets.

- Drawings, reports, PHA
- Plant worksheets
- Generic L$_{AS}$ definition tables
- Generic risk ranking matrix

Facilitator

- Completed facility worksheets
- Site-specific L$_{AS}$ level definition tables
- Site-specific risk ranking matrix

4. Site Survey

Surveying the Site

1. Review site drawings.
2. Review PHA results.
3. Review plant worksheets.
4. Complete plant survey/tour.

- Drawings, PHA
- Completed plant worksheets

Team

- Validated worksheets for physical protection, process control, safety/mitigation
- Shared information
- Security force worksheet

4

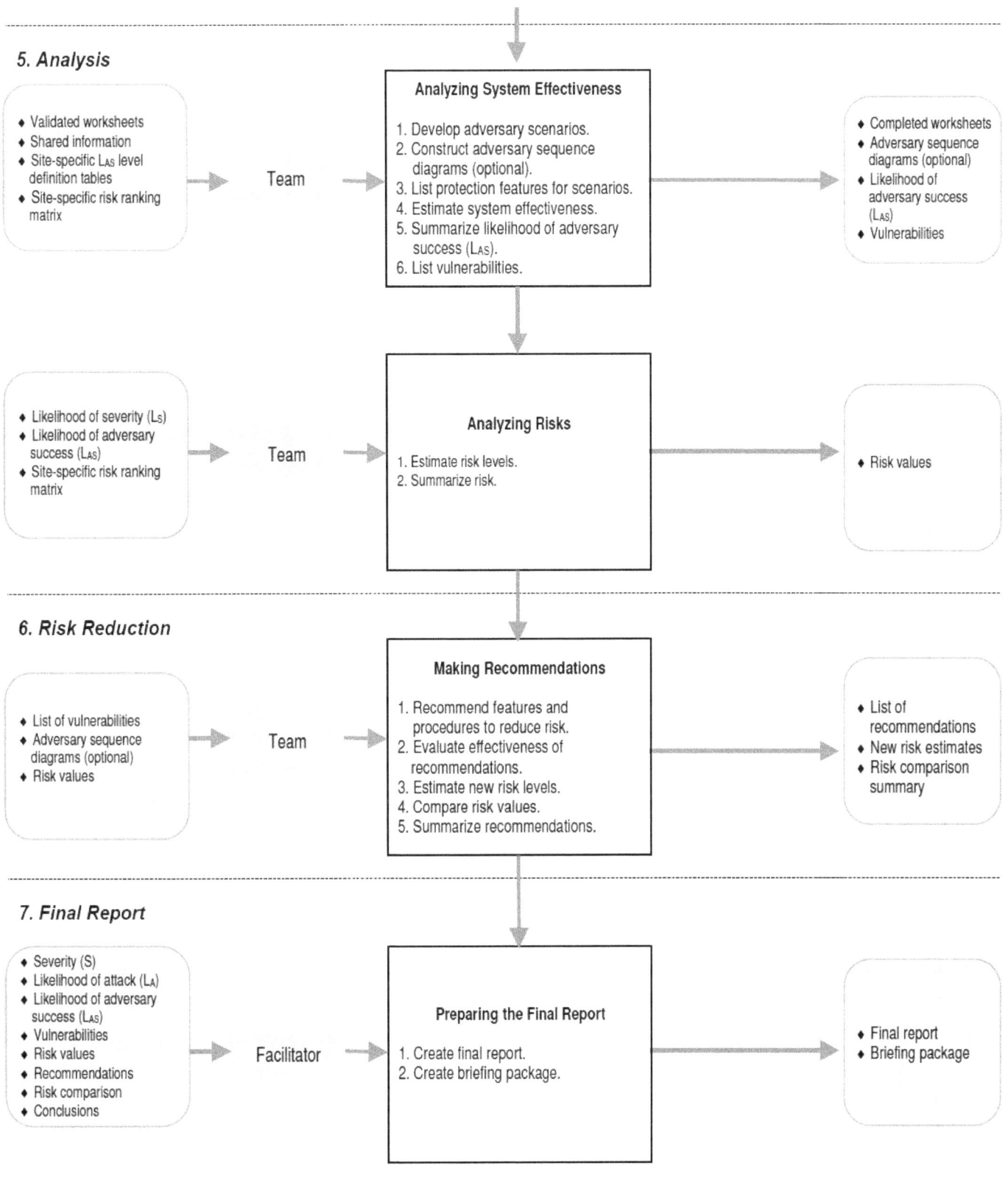

5. Analysis

Inputs:
- Validated worksheets
- Shared information
- Site-specific L_{AS} level definition tables
- Site-specific risk ranking matrix

Team

Analyzing System Effectiveness

1. Develop adversary scenarios.
2. Construct adversary sequence diagrams (optional).
3. List protection features for scenarios.
4. Estimate system effectiveness.
5. Summarize likelihood of adversary success (L_{AS}).
6. List vulnerabilities.

Outputs:
- Completed worksheets
- Adversary sequence diagrams (optional)
- Likelihood of adversary success (L_{AS})
- Vulnerabilities

Inputs:
- Likelihood of severity (L_S)
- Likelihood of adversary success (L_{AS})
- Site-specific risk ranking matrix

Team

Analyzing Risks

1. Estimate risk levels.
2. Summarize risk.

Outputs:
- Risk values

---

6. Risk Reduction

Inputs:
- List of vulnerabilities
- Adversary sequence diagrams (optional)
- Risk values

Team

Making Recommendations

1. Recommend features and procedures to reduce risk.
2. Evaluate effectiveness of recommendations.
3. Estimate new risk levels.
4. Compare risk values.
5. Summarize recommendations.

Outputs:
- List of recommendations
- New risk estimates
- Risk comparison summary

---

7. Final Report

Inputs:
- Severity (S)
- Likelihood of attack (L_A)
- Likelihood of adversary success (L_{AS})
- Vulnerabilities
- Risk values
- Recommendations
- Risk comparison
- Conclusions

Facilitator

Preparing the Final Report

1. Create final report.
2. Create briefing package.

Outputs:
- Final report
- Briefing package

1. Screening for the Need for a Vulnerability Assessment

Screening chemical facilities has two purposes:

- For individual CFs, the screening determines whether or not a vulnerability assessment (VA) should be conducted.

- For organizations with more than one CF, the screening determines which CFs should undergo VAs and prioritizes them.

The screening process is based primarily on the possible consequences of potential terrorist incidents at CFs.

The first question is, What is the desired event? For the information presented below, an offsite release was considered.

The second question is, Will the loss of a facility have a significant impact on the Nation (for example, Is it a sole source for a chemical vital to national defense industries)? If the answer is *yes,* the VA information may need to be classified.

The third question is, Does the facility have a total onsite inventory of threshold quantities (TQs) or greater of a chemical covered under Federal regulation 40 CFR 68.130? If the answer is *no,* a VA probably is not needed, although a CF may decide to do a VA for other reasons. For companies with more than one CF, the screening process should proceed to the other facilities. If the answer is *yes,* further screening is done based on the estimated number of people that would be affected by the worst-case scenario for the RMP, as shown in exhibit 2.

Exhibit 2: Further Screening Based on the Number of People That Would Be Affected by the Worst Case Scenario

---

Estimate how many people would be affected by the worst case scenario from the RMP for toxic substances and assign levels.

    1. More than 100,000
    2. 10,000–100,000
    3. 1,000–9,999
    4. Less than 1,000

Other factors considered in the screening step include accessibility, recognizability, and importance to the company, the region, and the Nation.

The final screening step is to prioritize the CFs that need VAs from level 1 (highest) to level 4 (lowest).

2. Defining the Project

After a CF has been screened and selected for a VA, the next step is to assign a facilitator trained in the VAM to define the VA project for that facility. Defining the project includes reviewing the purpose of the work to be performed, the tasks to be accomplished, and the resources to be allocated; creating a schedule of activities; and assembling a team to accomplish the work. The team may be the same one that prepared the process hazards analysis (PHA) for the facility, with the addition of one or more employees with security responsibilities. The project definition should be documented in a written statement that may be amended as the VA progresses.

3. Characterizing the Facility

An early step in security system analysis is to describe thoroughly the facility, including the site boundary, building locations, floor plans, access points, and physical protection features; and the processes that take place within the facility. This information can be obtained from several sources, including design blueprints, process descriptions, the PHA report, the RMP, the piping and instrument drawing (P&ID), and site surveys.

Characterize Facility Infrastructure and Processes

The characterization of a facility includes a description of building structures, traffic areas, infrastructure, terrain, weather conditions, and operational conditions. The first step is to gather information that will be helpful in identifying potential security vulnerabilities. The types of documentation include the following policy and procedure documents:

- Unusual occurrence reports.
- Existing threat assessment information.
- Results from past security surveys and audits.
- Building blueprints and plans for future structures.
- Site plans for detection, delay, and assessment systems.
- Operational procedures.

After the documentation has been collected, the following information should be extracted to characterize the facility. Site plans can help identify—

- Property borders.

- Entrance/exit routes to and from the facility, including—
  - Specific vulnerable areas in and around the facility, such as adjacent buildings that a sniper could use to target the building.

  - Adjacent parking lots and related security countermeasures.

  - Building locations and characteristics (for example, the purpose of the building, who is allowed access, and operational conditions or states).

  - Existing physical protection features.

- Access to the process control system.
  - List of authorized users.
  - Means and routes of access.
  - Protection features of the system.

Operational conditions are described by—

- The length and number of day and night shifts.

- Activities typical to each shift and the associated security implications.

- The number of employees, contractors, and visitors in the area during each shift and the level of access to the facility during weekdays, weekends, and holidays.

- The availability of security and safety personnel, including local law enforcement.

- Weather conditions for the region and time of the year.

- A description of adjacent residential or commercial areas.

- The use of batch versus continuous chemical processes.

Information on the facility structure includes the materials used in construction and the location and types of doors, gates, entryways, utilities, windows, and emergency exits.

Procedural information to be obtained includes—

- Entry control procedures to the facility for visitors, delivery persons, contractors, and vendors.

- Evacuation procedures.

- Emergency operations procedures in case of evacuation.

- Security procedures.

- Policies related to alarm assessment and communication to responding security personnel or local law enforcement.

- Safety procedures and features.

- Process control procedures and features.

To know how operations at the facility can be interrupted, it is necessary to know what is required for the site to operate effectively. The operation and location of equipment and safety features must be documented.

Determine List of Reportable Chemicals for Undesired Events

A list of reportable chemicals can be obtained from the PHA report. The processes for the reportable chemicals that pertain to the undesired events will be studied in detail.

Facility Characterization Matrix

The facility characterization matrix organizes the security factors for each processing activity and provides a framework for determining and prioritizing the critical activities (see exhibit 3).

Exhibit 3. Facility Characterization Matrix

No.	Parameter	Activity 1	Activity 2	Activity 3	Activity 4	Activity 5	Activity 6	Activity 7	Activity 8	Activity 9	Activity 10
1	Process activity										
2	Covered chemicals										
3	Quantity of covered chemicals								.		
4	Process duration										
5	Recognizability										
6	Accessibility										
7	Criticality rating (sum for activity)										

1. **Process activity.** Describe the activity (for example, from flow diagram, P&ID, reactor, pipe, storage tank, transportation).

2. **Covered chemicals.** Enter the names of all chemicals used in this activity. Enter *Y* if the chemical is listed in 40 CFR 68.130 or 29 CFR 1910.119. Enter *N* if the chemical is not listed.

3. **Quantity of covered chemicals.** Enter *1* if the quantity is more than 25 times the threshold quantity (TQ); *2* if the quantity is 10–25 times TQ; *3* if the quantity is 1–10 times TQ; and *4* if the quantity is TQ or less.

4. **Process duration.** Enter *1* if the process is 100% continuous; *2* if the process is 50–99% continuous; *3* if the process is 25–49% continuous; and *4* if the process is less than 25% continuous.

5. **Recognizability.** Enter *1* if the target and importance are clearly recognizable with little or no prior knowledge; *2* if the target and importance are easily recognizable with a small amount of prior knowledge; *3* if the target and importance are difficult to recognize without some prior knowledge; and *4* if the target and importance require extensive knowledge for recognition.

6. **Accessibility.** Enter *1* if easily accessible; *2* if fairly accessible (target is located outside or in an unsecured area); *3* if moderately accessible (target is located inside a building or enclosure); and *4* if not accessible or only accessible with extreme difficulty.

Determine critical activities: _____

The critical activity is the activity or activities with the lowest score under number 7 above.

Process Flow Diagram

A process flow diagram must be created that shows the use of each reportable chemical that can be exploited to create an undesired event. The diagram prepared for the PHA to determine the critical processing activities can be used for the VA as well. Exhibit 4 presents a sample process flow diagram.

Exhibit 4. Sample Process Flow Diagram

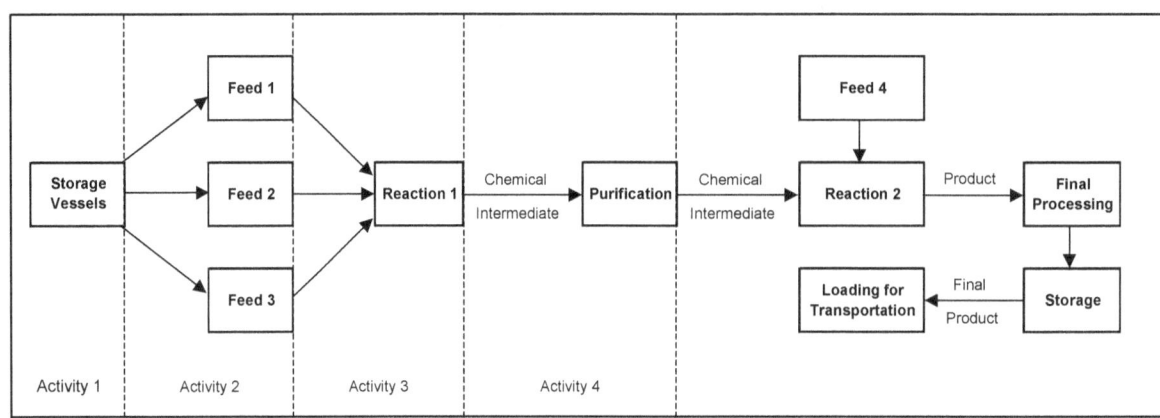

The chemical manufacturing process is divided into the following five stages, each of which may contain one or more processing activities: (1) When the chemical ingredients are incoming; (2) while the chemical ingredients are temporarily staged or stored awaiting use in production; (3) while the chemical product is in process; (4) while the chemical product is temporarily staged or stored awaiting shipment; and (5) when the chemical product is being shipped out. A chemical may not present a security hazard during all processing activities; for example, a hazardous chemical may be converted to a nonhazardous material during production. One way to determine which processing activities provide a potential for an undesired event (that is, critical activities), is to review the following attributes for each activity:

- The process activity underway.

- The specific chemicals being used and whether or not those chemicals are listed in 40 CFR 68.130 or 29 CFR 1910.119.

- The quantity, form, and concentration of the chemicals.

- The accessibility and recognizability of the chemicals.

- The potential for offsite release of the chemicals.

Once these attributes have been analyzed, the following types of measures related to facility security or protection against a chemical release or spill should also be reviewed:

- Physical protection measures.
- Process control protection measures.
- Active and passive measures to mitigate the harm resulting from a chemical spill or release.
- Plant safety measures.

10

Exhibit 5 presents a form for recording the use and handling of chemicals and the hazard reduction measures available at each stage in the manufacturing process. The information recorded can then be used to analyze the manufacturing process to determine the critical activities.

Exhibit 5. Form for Analysis of Operating Activities

	Manufacturing Steps				
	Incoming	Staging In	In Process	Staging Out	Outgoing
Use and handling of chemicals					
Manufacturing activities					
Regulated chemicals used*					
Quantity/form/concentration					
Location/duration					
Accessibility					
Recognizability					
Hazard reduction measures					
Physical protection					
Process control protection					
Active mitigation					
Passive mitigation					
Safety procedures					
*Chemicals or other hazardous substances listed in 40 CFR 68.130 or 29 CFR 1910.119.					

Process Control Flow Diagram

A flow diagram can be developed for the process control system for each critical activity. A generic process control flow diagram is provided in exhibit 6. Process control is normally a closed cycle in which a sensor provides information to a process control software application through a communications system. The application determines if the sensor information is within the predetermined (or calculated) data parameters and constraints. The results of this comparison are fed to an actuator, which controls the critical component. This feedback may control the component electronically or may indicate the need for a manual action. This closed-cycle process has many checks and balances to ensure that it stays safe. The investigation of how the process control can be subverted is likely to be extensive because all or part of the process control may be oral instructions to an individual monitoring the process. It may be fully computer controlled and automated, or it may be a hybrid in which only the sensor is automated and the action requires manual intervention. Further, some process control systems may use prior generations of hardware and software, while others are state of the art.

Exhibit 6. Generic Process Control

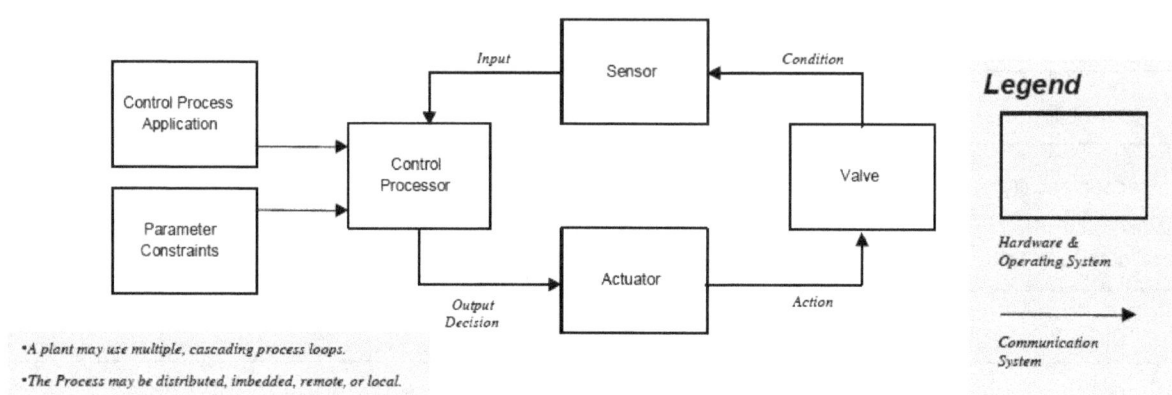

4. Deriving Severity Levels

The severity of consequences for each undesired event must be derived. For facilities that have conducted PHAs, the severity table created for the PHA should be considered first. This table may need to be modified to account for the consequences of a malevolent (rather than an accidental) event. Another source of data to help determine the severity of consequences is the analysis of the offsite consequences of the worst case and alternative-release scenarios. (The results of these analyses may also need to be modified.)

Exhibit 7 provides sample definitions of severity levels from 1 to 4. CFs that must submit RMPs most likely will be rated at severity level 1. The sample definitions below are most useful to CFs that do not have to submit RMPs but have decided to perform a VA. This table should be made site specific because various CFs and communities may assign different severity levels to similar consequences. Each undesired event will be assigned a severity level based on the consequences defined by the severity level definition table. This severity value (S) will be used in the risk analysis.

Exhibit 7. Sample Severity Level Definitions

S	Definition
1	Potential for any of the following resulting from a chemical release, detonation, or explosion: worker fatalities, public fatalities, extensive property damage, facility disabled for more than 1 month, major environmental impacts, or evacuation of neighbors.
2	Potential for any of the following resulting from a fire or major chemical release: nonfatal injuries, unit disabled for less than 1 month, or shutdown of road or river traffic.
3	Potential for any of the following resulting from a chemical release: unit evacuation, minor injuries, or minor offsite impact (for example, odor).
4	An operational problem that does not have potential to cause injury or a reportable chemical release with no offsite impact.

5. Assessing Threats

Describing the general threat. A general description of the threat is required to estimate the likelihood that adversaries might attempt an attack. This description includes the type of adversary and the tactics and capabilities (for example, the number in the group, weapons, equipment, and mode of transportation) associated with each threat.

Defining the site-specific threat. The threat also must be defined for each specific site. The definition includes the number of adversaries, their modus operandi, the type of tools and weapons they would use, and the type of events or acts they are willing to commit. It is important to update a site's threat analysis regularly, especially when obvious changes in threat occur.

Information Needed to Define Threat

Realistically, it is unlikely that CF personnel will have accurate knowledge of a specific threat beforehand. Therefore, judgments must be made in defining the threat. The more complete the available threat information is, the better those judgments will be.

The written definition of the threat is called the design basis threat (DBT). The type of information that is needed to describe a threat includes—

- The type of adversary.
- The adversary's potential actions.
- The adversary's motivations.
- The adversary's capabilities.

Adversaries can be divided into these three types: outsiders, insiders, and outsiders in collusion with insiders. Outsiders might include terrorists, criminals, extremists, gangs, or vandals. Insiders might include hostile, psychotic, or criminal employees or employees forced into cooperating with criminals by blackmail or threats of violence against them or their families.

A discussion of the adversary's potential actions must include what sorts of crimes these adversaries are interested in and capable of carrying out and which of these crimes could be committed against the specific site. Examples are theft, destruction, violence, and bombing.

Knowing the adversary's possible motivation can provide valuable information. Potential adversaries may undertake criminal actions because of ideological, economic, or personal motivations. Ideological motivations are linked to a political or philosophical system and include those of political terrorists, extremists, and radical environmentalists. Economic motivations involve a desire for financial gain, such as theft of hazardous materials for ransom, sale, or extortion. Personal motivations for committing a crime range from those of the hostile employee with a grievance against an employer or coworker to those of the psychotic individual.

The capability of the potential adversary is an important concern to the designer of a physical protection system. Factors in determining the adversary's capability include the following:

- The number of attackers.
- Their weapons and explosives.
- Their tools and equipment.
- Their means of transportation (for example, truck, helicopter, ultralight, or radio-controlled vehicle).
- Their technical skills and experience.
- Their knowledge of the facility and its operations.
- Possible insider assistance.

Information Collection

The types of organizations that may be contacted during the development of a DBT include local, State, and Federal law enforcement and intelligence agencies. Local authorities should be able to provide reports and source material on the type of criminal activities that are occurring and analytical projections of future activities. As an example, a special interest group may have previously only demonstrated at a facility but recently may have announced plans to commit acts of sabotage that would disrupt normal operations. Local periodicals, professional journals, the Internet, and other relevant materials should also be reviewed for reports of past incidents associated with the site.

Employee data should be reviewed for possible insider threats. The review should include the following:

- The number of personnel at the facility and their positions.

- The number of direct employees versus the number of contractors, visitors, and vendors.

- Any problems that have occurred with direct or contract employees (for example, domestic violence problems, union disputes, and downsizing).

An example of the result of the information collection is shown in exhibit 8. This threat information is used to develop adversary scenarios and estimate the effectiveness of the protection system.

Exhibit 8. Sample Site-Specific Threat Description

Type of Adversary	Number	Equipment	Vehicle	Weapon	Tactic
Terrorist outsider (may include an insider colluding)	2–3	Handtools Power tools Body armor Chemicals Biological agents	4x4 All-terrain vehicles Pickup trucks Aircraft	Handguns Automatics Explosives	Cause catastrophic events Theft
Criminal	2–3	Handtools Body armor	Foot Truck Aircraft	Handguns Explosives	Extortion Theft
Extremist	5–10	Signs Chains Locks Handtools	Cars Buses	No weapons	Protests Civil disobedience Damage Destruction
Insider	1	Onsite equipment	Cars Pickup trucks 4x4	Handguns Automatics Explosives	Destruction Violence Theft
Vandal	1–3	Paint	Cars Pickup trucks	Hunting rifles	Random shootings Tagging

Likelihood of attack (L_A). After the threat spectrum has been described, the information can be used together with statistics of past events and site-specific perceptions of threats to categorize threats in terms of likelihood that each would attempt an undesired event. The Department of Defense (DoD) standard definitions[1] have been modified for use in categorizing the threats against CFs, as shown in exhibit 9.

Exhibit 9. Definitions of Level of Likelihood of Attack (L_A)

L_A	Definition
1	Threat exists, is capable, has intent or history, and has targeted the facility.
2	Threat exists, is capable, has intent or history, but has not targeted the facility.
3	Threat exists and is capable, but has no intent or history and has not targeted the facility.
4	Threat exists, but is not capable of causing undesired event.

6. Prioritizing Cases

After the severity (S) of each undesired event and the likelihood of attack (L_A) for each adversary group have been determined, these values are ranked in a matrix (exhibit 10) to derive the L_S values. If, for example, an adversary group has a level 2 likelihood of attack for a specific undesired event and the undesired event has a severity level of 3, the likelihood and severity level (L_S) would be 3. Priority cases would be those undesired event/adversary group pairs with a likelihood and severity (L_S) value closer to 1 than the value chosen by the CF. These priority cases should be analyzed further for protection system effectiveness.

Exhibit 10. Sample Likelihood and Severity Priority Ranking Matrix

L_S	Severity of Consequences (S)			
	1	2	3	4
1	1	1	2	4
2	1	2	3	4
3	2	3	4	4
4	3	4	4	4

(Likelihood of Attack (L_A) labels the rows: 1, 2, 3, 4)

7. Preparing for Site Analysis

To prepare for the analysis to determine the effectiveness of the site protection system, background information should be assembled. This information should include site drawings, the PHA, physical protection system (PPS) features, and process control data. Information worksheets have been developed to collect site information needed for the effectiveness analysis and documentation.[2]

Physical Protection System

An effective security system must be able to detect the adversary and delay it long enough for a response force to arrive and neutralize it before the mission is accomplished.

Detection. The discovery of adversary action, which includes sensing covert or overt actions, must be preceded by the following events:

- A sensor (equipment or personnel) reacts to an abnormal occurrence and initiates an alarm.
- Information from the sensor and assessment subsystems is reported and displayed.
- Someone assesses the information and determines the alarm to be valid or invalid.

16

Methods of detection include a wide range of technologies and personnel. Entry control—a means of allowing entry of authorized personnel and detecting the attempted entry of unauthorized personnel and contraband—is part of the detection function of physical protection. Entry control works best when entry is permitted only through several layers of protection that surround targets of malevolent attacks. Entry to each layer should be controlled to filter and progressively reduce the population that has access. Only individuals who need direct access to the target should be allowed through the final entry control point. Searching for metal (possible weapons or tools) and explosives (possible bombs or breaching charges) is required for high-security areas. This may be accomplished using metal detectors, x-ray screeners (for packages), and explosive detectors. Security personnel at fixed posts or on patrol may serve a vital role in detecting an intrusion. Other personnel can contribute to detection if they are trained in security concerns and have a means to alert the security force in the event of a problem.

An effective detection alarm assessment system provides information about whether the alarm is valid or a nuisance and details about the cause of the alarm. The effectiveness of the detection function is measured both by the probability of sensing adversary action and by the time required for reporting and assessing the alarm.

Delay. Delay can be accomplished by fixed or active barriers (for example, doors, vaults, and locks) or by sensor-activated barriers (for example, dispensed liquids and foams). Entry control, to the extent it includes locks, may also be a delaying factor. Security personnel can be considered an element of delay if they are in fixed and well-protected positions.

The measure of delay effectiveness is the time required by the adversary (after detection) to bypass each delay element.

Response. Actions taken by the security response force (usually onsite security personnel or local law enforcement officers) can prevent adversarial success. Response consists of interruption and neutralization. Interruption is not only stopping the adversary's progress; it also includes communicating accurate information about adversarial actions to the response force and deploying the response force.

The effectiveness measures for response communication are the probability of accurate communication and the time required to communicate with the response force. Neutralization is the act of stopping the adversary before the goal is accomplished. The effectiveness measures for neutralization are security police force equipment, training, tactics, cover capabilities, and engagement effectiveness. The measure of overall response effectiveness is the time between the receipt of a communication of adversarial actions and the interruption and neutralization of the action.

In addition to the elements described above, an effective PPS has these specific characteristics:

- Protection in depth.
- Minimum consequence of component failure.
- Balanced protection.

Protection in Depth

Protection in depth means that an adversary should be required to avoid or defeat several protective devices in sequence to accomplish its goal. For example, an adversary might have to penetrate three separate barriers before gaining entry to a process control room. The effectiveness of each barrier and the time required to penetrate them may differ, but each requires a separate and distinct act as the adversary moves along the planned path.

Minimum Consequence of Component Failure

Every complex system will have a component failure at some time. Causes of component failure in a PPS can range from environmental factors, which may be expected, to adversary actions beyond the scope of the threat used in the system design. Although it is important to know the cause of component failure to restore the system to normal operation, it is more important that contingency plans be provided so the system can continue to operate.

Balanced Protection

Balanced protection means that no matter how adversaries attempt to accomplish their goals, they will encounter effective elements of the PPS. In a completely balanced system, all barriers would take the same time to penetrate and would have the same probability of detecting penetration. However, complete balance is probably not possible or desirable; there is no advantage to overdesigning a PPS.

All of the hardware elements of the system must be installed, maintained, and operated properly. The procedures of the PPS must be compatible with the procedures of the facility. Security, safety, and operational objectives must be accomplished at all times.

Determination of L_{AS}

As discussed above, an effective PPS will neutralize the adversary and prevent an undesired event with a high degree of confidence. The more effective the PPS, the less likely the adversary will succeed. Thus L_{AS} is derived directly from estimates of the PPS effectiveness, as shown in the definition table (exhibit 11). The facilitator should develop a definition table for the levels of likelihood of adversary success for the physical protection system that is specific to the site.

Exhibit 11. Sample Definitions of Likelihood of Adversary Success (L_{AS})

L_{AS}	Definition
1	Ineffective or no protection measures; catastrophic event is expected.
2	Few protection measures; catastrophic event is probable.
3	Major protection measures; catastrophic event is possible.
4	Complete protection measures; catastrophic event is prevented.

Protection System for Process Control

Only an overview of the computer and electronic process control systems at CFs was completed in conjunction with the project that developed the prototype CF VAM. Consequently, the protection system analysis for computer and electronic process control systems presented in this methodology should not be considered complete. In performing the protection system analysis for a CF, review of the Process Flow Diagram (exhibit 4) may help identify locations in addition to those presented here where the process control system should intersect with the process flow.

An effective protection system for process control protects all of the critical functions of the system and their interfaces, including, but not limited to—

- Communications.
- Commercial hardware and software.
- Application software.
- Parameter data.
- Support infrastructure; for example, power and heating, ventilation, and air conditioning (HVAC).

If one of these functions is not adequately protected, the adversary could exploit that function to use the process control system to cause the undesired event. In the worst case scenario, the adversary would not even have to come onsite to trigger the event. The definition table for the likelihood of adversary success (L_{AS}) (exhibit 11) also can be applied to the critical functions of the process control system.

The final step of preparing for the system effectiveness analysis is to create a priority ranking matrix that combines likelihood and severity of attack (L_S) (the matrix for which is presented in exhibit 10) and likelihood of adversary success (L_{AS}) (see exhibit 12). The completed matrix will be used to estimate risk levels.

Exhibit 12. Sample Risk Priority Ranking Matrix

Risk	Likelihood of Adversary Success (L_{AS})			
Likelihood and Severity of of Attack (L_S)	1	2	3	4
1	1	1	2	4
2	1	2	3	4
3	2	3	4	4
4	3	4	4	4

Mitigation

When the protection system cannot prevent an undesired event, mitigation features can reduce consequences, thus reducing risk. Mitigation features range from sensors that cause systems to shut down and assume a fail-safe condition if a problem is detected to early warning systems that alert first responders. (Note: Mitigation measures may be disabled by adversaries.)

8. Surveying the Site

The information, drawings, and worksheets that were assembled and completed by the facilitator should be reviewed by the entire team for accuracy and validation in preparation for the system effectiveness analysis that follows. A walk-through survey of the site should be done with special emphasis on verifying critical activities and target information.

9. Analyzing the System's Effectiveness

Estimating system effectiveness means judging whether the protection features of the facility are adequate to prevent the undesired event from occurring. For each critical activity, two or more estimates of protection system effectiveness will be made: One or more for the physical protection system and one or more for the protection system for process control. For the physical protection system, the first estimate measures the system's effectiveness in preventing the undesired event. If the undesired event cannot be prevented, another estimate measures the system's effectiveness in detecting the event and mitigating its consequences so that the event is not catastrophic.

For each undesired event or adversary group, the steps for estimating the effectiveness of the physical protection system are—

- Specifying the most vulnerable adversary scenario—a physical path.

- Listing the features of the facility that are designed to protect against the scenario.

- Determining a likelihood of adversary success (L_{AS}) level for the scenario from the definition table (exhibit 11).

For each undesired event or adversary group, the steps for estimating the effectiveness of the process control protection system are—

- Specifying the most vulnerable adversary scenario—a process control path.

- Listing the features of the process control system that are designed to protect against the scenario.

- Determining a likelihood of adversary success (L_{AS}) level for the scenario from the definition table (exhibit 11).

Most Vulnerable Adversary Scenario—A Physical Path

The first step in determining the most vulnerable adversary scenarios is to consider adversary strategies. The adversary will try to attack the plant or disrupt the chemical manufacturing process at its most vulnerable point. Team members will identify the most vulnerable points of the facility and the plant processes based on their knowledge of the site, its operations, and its existing protection system.

Several factors must be considered in determining the most vulnerable points of attack:

- Protection system weaknesses noted on data collection worksheets and the site survey.
  - Least-protected system features (for example, detection, delay, response, or mitigation).
  - Easiest system features to defeat.
  - Worst consequences.

- Facility operating states or environmental conditions that the adversary could use to an advantage.
  - Emergency conditions.
  - No personnel onsite.
  - Inclement weather.

After the most vulnerable adversary strategies for each undesired event have been established, adversary paths to the critical assets to cause that event are considered. Site layout drawings may help summarize all possible physical paths from outside the facility into areas that house critical assets. Exhibit 13 illustrates a layout drawing with possible adversary paths.

Exhibit 13. Possible Adversary Paths

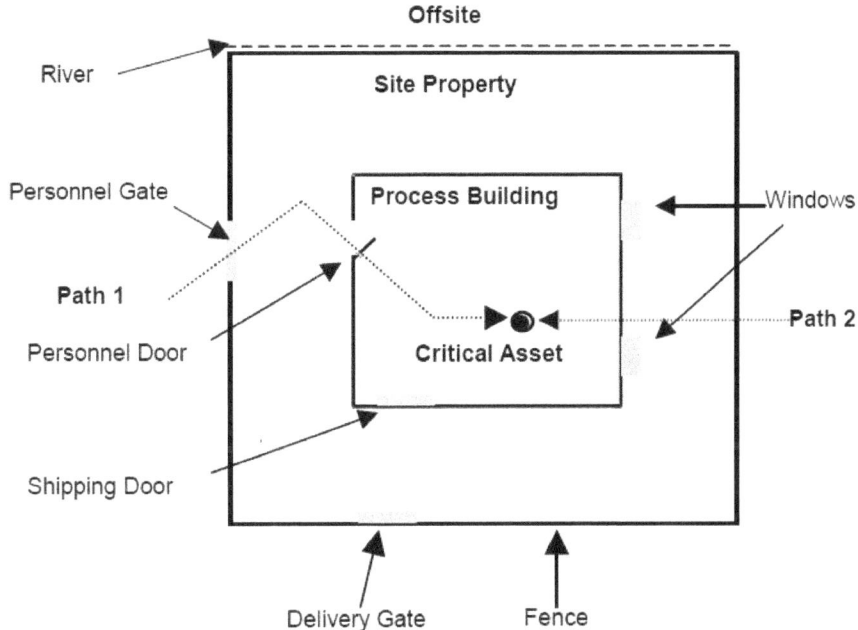

The adversary sequence diagram (ASD), which models the facility's physical protection system, identifies paths that adversaries can follow to commit sabotage or theft. ASDs help prevent overlooking possible adversary paths and help identify protection system upgrades that affect the paths most vulnerable to adversaries. Exhibit 14 presents an ASD for the facility shown in exhibit 13. The most vulnerable adversary path is used to measure the effectiveness of the physical protection system.

Exhibit 14. Sample Facility Adversary Sequence Diagram

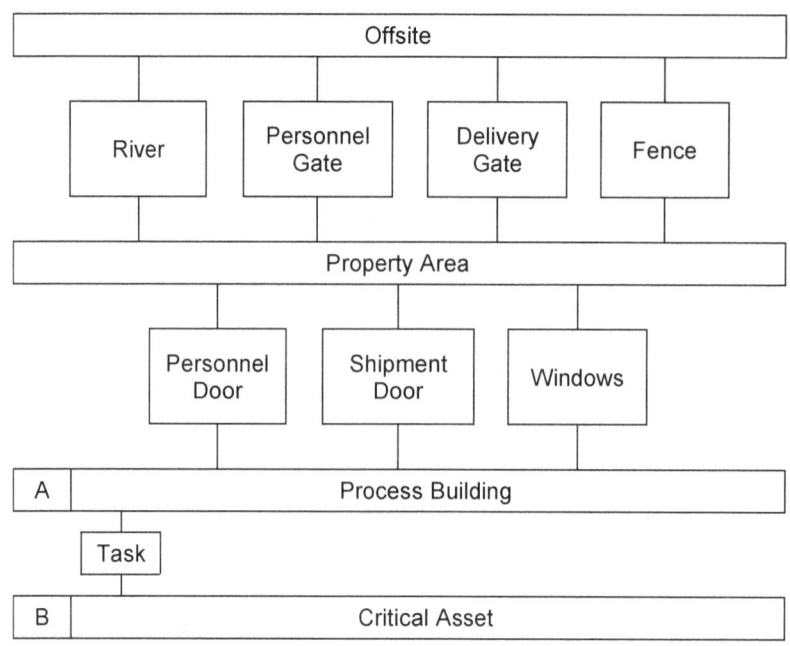

From the most vulnerable strategies and physical paths postulated, the team should specify a most-vulnerable adversary scenario. More than one scenario can be analyzed. The scenarios are used to determine the effectiveness of the protection system.

Physical Protection Features for Scenario

The features of the facility that support the functions of detection, delay, response, and mitigation and any safety features that could affect the outcome of the adversary scenario should be noted. These features can be identified from the facility worksheets used to determine the system's effectiveness, the characterization matrix, and facility personnel's knowledge of such features. Exhibit 15 presents a sample adversary scenario and lists site features for each system function.

Exhibit 15. Sample Scenario and Protection System Features

Most Vulnerable Scenario: Adversary climbs over property fence, enters process building
via open rollup doors, traverses to critical asset, and destroys equipment.

Detection Features	Delay Features	Response Features	Mitigation/ Safety Features
• Security officer personnel entrance • Camera surveillance of building perimeter • Personnel during working hours • Process sensors	• Property fence—6-foot chain link • Standard doors and locks	• Local law enforcement can respond in 30 minutes • Personnel during working hours	• Process safety controls

Likelihood of Adversary Success for Scenario—Physical

Using the list of features for each PPS element together with the definition table for likelihood of adversary success (L_{AS}) (exhibit 11), the assessment team determines a likelihood of adversary success level for each scenario. The team should first consider if the PPS features would be expected to prevent the undesired event. If the expectation is low, the team considers whether detection combined with mitigation measures would reduce the consequences of undesired events to acceptable levels.

For example, assume a team decides that for the scenario in exhibit 14, the levels of detection, delay, and response are low, and therefore the protection system cannot prevent the undesired event. Further, assume that the team judges the mitigation/safety function to be at the medium level. Because the detection function is low, the system effectiveness in preventing a catastrophic event is low. Using the definitions in exhibit 11, the likelihood of adversary success (L_{AS}) for this scenario is rated at 2. This level is then used in the matrix (exhibit 12) to estimate the risk level for physical protection for the activity.

Whenever protection system effectiveness is low, specific system functions should be reviewed and vulnerabilities identified and addressed.

Most Vulnerable Adversary Scenario—A Process Control Path

The possible process control adversary paths can be reviewed on the facility process flow diagram (exhibit 4). As for the physical paths, the assessment team should specify what they believe to be the most vulnerable adversary scenario that would cause the undesired event using the process control system.

The analysis should consider not only the prevention of an undesired event, but also the ability of process control (or the lack of process control) to eliminate or mitigate the harms.

Protection for Process Control Scenario

The features of the process control protection system that could affect the outcome of the adversary scenario should be noted. As with the physical protection system, these features can be identified from facility worksheets used to evaluate the system's effectiveness, the characterization matrix, and facility personnel's knowledge of the features. The system must protect the process control features mentioned in the section on preparing the site analysis: communications, commercial hardware and software, application software, and parameter data or support infrastructure (for example, power and HVAC). Exhibit 16 proposes a process control adversary scenario and lists process control features that can protect against that scenario.

Exhibit 16. Sample Process Control Protection Features

Most Vulnerable Process Control Scenario:
Adversary accesses process control system via the Internet

Communications	Commercial Hardware and Software	Application Software	Parameter Data	Support Infrastructure
• Encryption • Lock and sensor communications rooms • Supervised lines • Authentication • Redundant systems	• Current security patches • Strong passwords • Audits • Monitoring unusual use	• Configuration control • Trusted source • Documentation • Thorough testing	• Validate value and effect • Configuration control • Read only • Authenticate written privilege	• Uninterruptable power supply • Automatic switch to backup • Environmental controls

Likelihood of Adversary Success for Process Control Scenario

The assessment team must judge the effectiveness of the process control system protections in preventing the adversary from using the system to cause the undesired event. The likelihood of adversary success level (LAS) and the risk level can be determined using the definition table (exhibit 11) and matrix (exhibit 12). If any of these systems—communications, commercial hardware and software, application software, parameter data, or support infrastructure—can be exploited, the system effectiveness is low and vulnerabilities are implied. In addition, reviewing the features lacking in any process control protection categories may identify specific vulnerabilities that should be addressed when making recommendations.

10. Analyzing Risks

A brief review of the methodology is presented below in preparation for risk analysis.

For the purposes of this methodology,

> Risk is a function of S, L_A, and L_{AS}
> S = severity of consequences of an event (section 4).
> L_A = likelihood of adversary attack (section 5).
> L_S = likelihood of adversary attack and severity of consequences of an event (section 6).
> L_{AS} = likelihood of adversary success in causing a catastrophic event (section 9).

Priority cases for an undesired event or adversary group were determined by estimating the likelihood and severity level (L_S) using the priority ranking matrix for likelihood of attack (L_A) and severity (S) (see exhibit 10). L_S levels are combined with L_{AS} levels to estimate the level of risk for each undesired event/adversary group (see exhibit 12). Exhibit 17 is a flowchart for the process, and exhibit 18 summarizes the results of the risk analysis.

Exhibit 17. Risk Analysis Flowchart

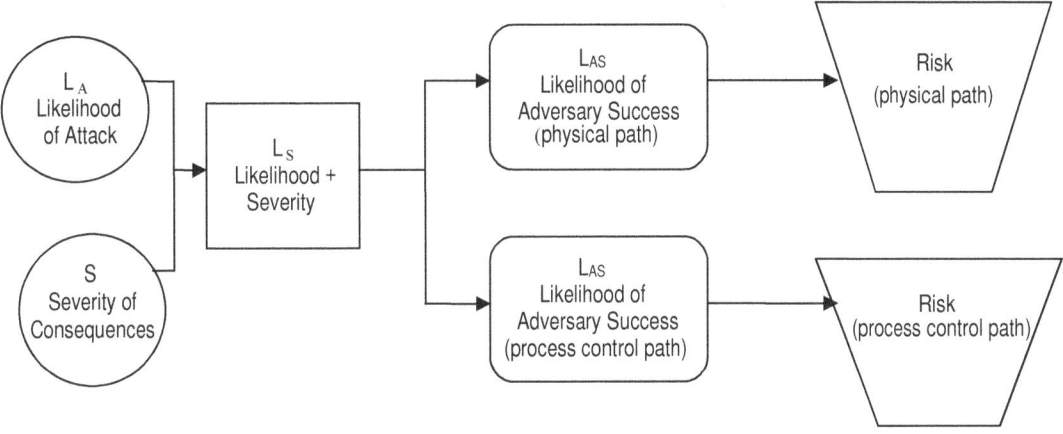

Exhibit 18. Risk Level Summary

Risk Level Summary	Undesired Event = _____ Severity (S) = _____					
	Adversary Group	L_S	L_{AS} (physical)	Risk (physical)	L_{AS} (process control)	Risk (process control)
Activity 1						
Activity 2						
Activity 3						

If the risk level is 1, 2, or 3 for any adversary group, the risk should be decreased. Recommendations to reduce the risk should address specific vulnerabilities identified in section 9.

11. Making Recommendations for Risk Reduction

If the risk level is 1, 2, or 3, detection, delay, response, and mitigation/safety features that eliminate or mitigate the specific identified vulnerabilities should be suggested. The goal is low-cost, high-return upgrades. Upgrade features should provide—

- Protection for common vulnerabilities.
- Protection in depth.
- Balanced protection.

Upgrading vulnerabilities common to all undesired events should be considered first because this can result in greater protection against many scenarios. Guidance on where to place specific features would ask: 1) Where is it most desirable to have the first detection point? and 2) Where would added delay prevent or lessen the likelihood of worst case scenarios? In general, the first detection point must be as early as possible, but placing the delay and response/mitigation features closer to a target could provide the most benefit if all paths are affected. The site layout plan or an ASD, if developed, can guide decisions about where features should be placed.

Protection in depth forces an adversary to avoid or defeat several protective devices in sequence. Layers of features cause difficulties for an adversary, including increased uncertainty about the system, the requirement for more extensive preparations prior to the attack, and additional steps where failure could occur.

Balanced protection ensures that an adversary will encounter effective elements of the physical protection system no matter how the critical asset is approached. For a completely balanced layer of system features, the detection performances and delay times are equal along all ASD paths. Complete balance is probably not possible. Some features may have inherent protection characteristics. Walls, for example, may resist penetration because of structural or safety requirements. Thus, door, hatch, and grill delays may be less than wall delays and still be adequate. There is no advantage to overdesigning specific features that result in unbalanced protection. For example, it is pointless to install a costly vault door on a flimsy wall. Reviewing the site layout plan or the ASD will help ensure all adversary paths are protected.

Recommendations may include:

- Physical protection improvements (detection, delay, and response improvements); for example:
  - Sensors on gates and doors.
  - An assessment system (cameras).
  - A security alarm control center.
  - Hardened doors and locks.
  - Access control (cards + PIN) on doors and gates.
  - A compartmentalized facility.

- Consequence reduction improvements (detection, mitigation improvements); for example:
  - Reduction of quantity of controlled chemicals (to less than TQ).
  - Dispersion of chemicals (in storage).
  - Addition of mitigation measures conceived or known by facility personnel.

- Process control protection improvements; for example:
  - Chemical/process sensors routed to alarm control center.
  - Protected and strong passwords that are changed regularly.
  - Firewalls.
  - Configuration control (of security patches/routing table/control parameters).
  - Virus protection.
  - Computer audits of activity on network.
  - Encryption and authentication.
  - Emergency backups/backup power.
  - Redundant communication.
  - Process control isolated from external information systems.

After recommendations are made, the new system effectiveness level and risk level should be estimated. The process continues until acceptable risk levels (probably 3 or 4) are achieved. Other effects of the recommendations—such as cost, impact on operations or schedules, and employee acceptance—should also be considered.

12. Preparing the Final Report

The final report and package for briefing management can be prepared from the worksheets when completing the analysis. Items suggested for inclusion in the final report are—

1. Screening process results.
2. Facility characterization matrix and critical activities analyzed.
3. Severity level definition table and severity level for each undesired event.
4. Threat definition table.
5. Likelihood of attack level definition table and L_A levels for each undesired event/adversary group.
6. L_S (likelihood and severity) priority ranking matrix and L_S levels for each undesired event/adversary group.
7. Priority undesired event/adversary groups analyzed.
8. Most vulnerable adversary scenarios for both physical and process control paths for each priority undesired event/adversary group.
9. L_{AS} definition table and L_{AS} levels for both physical and process control paths for each priority undesired event/adversary group.
10. Risk priority ranking matrix and risk levels for both physical and process control paths for each priority undesired event/adversary group (risk level summary table).
11. Recommendations to reduce risk levels.

Notes

[1] Shelton, Henry H., Chairman of the Joint Chiefs of Staff, Joint Pub. 3–07.2, "Joint Tactics, Techniques and Procedures for Antiterrorism," March 17, 1998 (2d ed.). Available on the World Wide Web at http://www.dtic.mil/doctrine/jel/new_pubs/jp3_07_2.pdf.

[2] Information about the worksheets is available from Cal Jaeger, principal member of technical staff, Sandia National Laboratories. Mr. Jaeger can be reached by telephone at 505–844–4986 or by e-mail at cdjaege@sandia.gov.

About the National Institute of Justice

NIJ is the research, development, and evaluation agency of the U.S. Department of Justice and is solely dedicated to researching crime control and justice issues. NIJ provides objective, independent, nonpartisan, evidence-based knowledge and tools to meet the challenges of crime and justice, particularly at the State and local levels. NIJ's principal authorities are derived from the Omnibus Crime Control and Safe Streets Act of 1968, as amended (42 U.S.C. §§ 3721–3723).

The NIJ Director is appointed by the President and confirmed by the Senate. The NIJ Director establishes the Institute's objectives, guided by the priorities of the Office of Justice Programs, the U.S. Department of Justice, and the needs of the field. The Institute actively solicits the views of criminal justice and other professionals and researchers to inform its search for the knowledge and tools to guide policy and practice.

NIJ's Mission

NIJ's mission is to advance scientific research, development, and evaluation to enhance the administration of justice and public safety.

NIJ's Strategic Goals and Program Areas

NIJ has seven strategic goals grouped into three categories:

Creating relevant knowledge and tools:

1. Partner with State and local practitioners and policymakers to identify social science research and technology needs.

2. Create scientific, relevant, and reliable knowledge—with a particular emphasis on violent crime, drugs and crime, cost-effectiveness, and community-based efforts—to enhance the administration of justice and public safety.

3. Develop affordable and effective tools and technologies to enhance the administration of justice and public safety.

Dissemination:

4. Disseminate relevant knowledge and information to practitioners and policymakers in an understandable, timely, and concise manner.

5. Act as an honest broker to identify the information, tools, and technologies that respond to the needs of stakeholders.

Agency management:

6. Practice fairness and openness in the research and development process.

7. Ensure professionalism, excellence, accountability, cost-effectiveness, and integrity in the management and conduct of NIJ activities and programs.

NIJ's Structure

NIJ has three operating units. The Office of Research and Evaluation manages social science research and evaluation and crime mapping research. The Office of Science and Technology manages technology research and development, standards development, and technology assistance to State and local law enforcement and corrections agencies. The Office of Development and Communications manages field tests of model programs, international research, and knowledge dissemination programs. NIJ is a component of the Office of Justice Programs, which also includes the Bureau of Justice Assistance, the Bureau of Justice Statistics, the Office of Juvenile Justice and Delinquency Prevention, and the Office for Victims of Crime.

To find out more about the National Institute of Justice, please contact:

National Criminal Justice
  Reference Service
P.O. Box 6000
Rockville, MD 20849–6000
800–851–3420
e-mail: *askncjrs@ncjrs.org*

To obtain an electronic version of this document, access the NIJ Web site (*http://www.ojp.usdoj.gov/nij*).

If you have questions, call or e-mail NCJRS.